Always the Blue Tide Turning

# Always the Blue Tide Turning

Poems by

Mary Shay McGuire

Cover design by Shay Culligan
Cover art "Writing Desk" by Mary Shay McGuire

ISBN: 978-1-952326-19-6

Kelsay Books
502 South 1040 East, A-119
American Fork, Utah, 84003

For my father
James Patrick McGuire
who bought me my first book of poetry

I give thanks to my daughters Abigail Elizabeth
and Anne Catherine, my mother who recited poetry
to me, my aunt Mary Shay, to Carol Motta and
Mary Rohrer-Dann, and to editor Sarah Russell,
who helped these poems become a book.

# Acknowledgments

*Ariel Chart:* Bittersweet Vines, My Mother, My Brother

*Eclectica:* My Grandmother's Apartment

*Literary Heist:* Remember, reprinted in *Literary Yard*

*Literary Yard:* Driving to the Ocean, Osborne Street, Fall River, Massachusetts, Fall River Song

*The Drabble:* The First Week, The Shadow of the Summer

*The Hackney National Award for Poetry:* Credo

*Uppagus:* Memorial Day, Tuesday After Memorial Day

*Vita Brevis:* Daisy Fleabane, I Miss the Twilight Nights, Peony petals slowly open, Seeds

# Awards

AWP Award for Creative Nonfiction, published in *Quarterly West*

Nominated by The Pennsylvania State University for the AWP
Award for Creative Nonfiction

The Hackney National Award for Poetry for "Credo"

American Academy of Poets, second prize

The New Millennium Prize for Poetry

# Contents

# III

I

# Peony petals slowly open

roses close tight at twilight
it has happened
it will happen again

I smell the snow in winter
suddenly I am a child again
in a wool cap in New England

the cat's coat is black luxury
once I found a cat
someday I will find another

# The Shadow of the Summer

evening sun slants
across June grass
that moment
the sun lowering
sending streams of light
repeating, repeating
each time carrying me back

to Massachusetts childhood
near the wide Taunton River
near the Atlantic Ocean
where you run to the sea
watch the tides forever
pulling in, pulling out

that June evening sun's shadow
I remember—crosses the lawn
the moment I hold my father's hand
my mother bends taking our picture
as if everything is fine

# Fall River Song

I need to tell you
about the house
on the steepest hill
where I grew up
its shingles and gray trim
its rooms breathing light

my mother prayed
each night on her knees
to the Infant of Prague
on some late afternoons
she painted her nails red
by the double windows
looking to the Taunton River
to the eight-block hill
and scruff—North Park
its shallow, gritty ice pond
its Snake Hill
where lovers parked

I need to tell you
I think of the end of the park so far
below with forty stone steps
and St. Joseph's church
dark and candled far beyond
the grim confessional every Saturday
mass each Sunday, the navy blazers,
the strict march
of holy days and holidays
abstaining from meat, fasting
the thought of white heaven
of pointy red flamed hell

and yet I yearn for the scent
of white wax flaming,
tilted candles lit in the dark church—
sure transporters of prayer—
the May processions singing with adoration
strewing flowers, begging grace

I remember the ache of that love
that light of grace shining through the trees

# One summer night


my father glided the car
rounding the arch
of the semi-circle
to the entrance of the restaurant
with its many open-shuttered windows
and large lawns that reached to far trees
at the doorway a gaggle of tanned
laughing teenage boys
volleyed to valet the car

I felt I glided up the steps
that spilled from the doorway
and then seated near a window whose view
opened toward the bay and further to the sea
(years later I'd see how my father slipped
carefully folded bills to the maître d')

I looked at the liquidy
silver knives and forks
the antique chairs
the entrees in scrolled script
my mother toyed with the edge of her napkin

now the beginning of their martini hour
the pungent aroma of the gin
the thick liquid lingering on glass
the sweet smell of raw bar—
oysters on the half shell, little necks
white wine sacred to the sole
the voices rose and my father laughed more
my brother looked out the window
my little sister cried
everything took too long

near the end I wandered
out into the vast
side parking lot
crushed with clam shells
climbing into the back seat
I fell into slumber
wakened by a voice of anger
the gaiety gone, the liquor holding its own

# My Grandmother's Apartment

*In Fall River, Massachusetts the lumbering three-tiered tenements were
called Irish Battleships. The apartments became smaller as the building
soared. Each floor was a replica of the other—only tinier, like a layered
cake reaching up and up.*


I loved my grandmother's apartment
following the curving steps
to the large kitchen with a table near the windows
where I watched her make perfect pies
as she dotted the crust with butter and cream
I loved the gas stove
its pilot light—an amber-blue flame—
the pantry with high glass-door cupboards
the dining room where she sewed
and begonias and lacey leafed shamrocks
bloomed year round on her window sills

some Saturdays I would sneak through
the parlor used only at Christmas,
funerals or winter Sunday afternoons
when odd, unknown cousins came
and sat on the stiff horsehair sofa
and two maroon side chairs
their arms covered with crocheted doilies

I loved to spend the night in the bedroom
with carved pineapples topping
the high post twin beds
and on the wall a framed print
of a red, luscious strawberry
that later my grandmother told me
was the Sacred Heart of Christ
coiled not with vines but thorns

# Osborne Street, Fall River, Massachusetts

of the men that flirted, winked and laughed
of the men that teased that she was a woman at four
of the boy who wanted to touch
of the boy who wanted to show
of the mothers who tied their daughter's
  braids in tight twined thread
of the mother who slept
of the nuns who wore black
of the railed hill that was too steep
of the father returned from the war
  in the new green Buick
of the brother beginning to break
of the times to remember this
  again and again

# Driving to the Ocean

all it takes is a white clapboard house
on a winding road
and I am back
I am seven
in the backseat of the car seeing

scrubby fields, rusty trucks
then the land begins to open
the sun on white here and there houses

the daggered leaves of Irish Bells on lonely
once-were-mansion grounds
its road whispered about each time
where long ago a girl's raped
dead body had been found

wild flowers and sometimes orange day lilies
that the grownups say we can stop
and pick on the way back
and never do

the yard with a pet monkey in a red skirt
tethered on a long rope to a lone tree
her nimble fingers holding an apple
that she gnaws in monkey delight

then woods, gentle woods
with sunlight streaming through
and a river, a quiet river

then a hill
crests
gulls raucous overhead
and, by God, we see water so blue
we all laugh and laugh and laugh

# My Mother, My Brother

as we walked toward
our Cape Cod cottage
my mother drew
me to the side yard
she bent to touch,
to name each herb
thyme, chives,
borage, basil
then she paused—
her faintest touch on the sea foam,
an airy fluff of herb—pale and green
suds of broken waves
foaming at the edge of the garden,

then I knew the family summerhouse
belonged to my mother and my brother
together they had bought it
I felt afraid and stayed afraid,
afraid, all these years
of their closed union

# Slower than Death

my brother phones to say
the white pine I planted from seed
towers over his cottage
he taunts, *are you sure you planted it?*

and, *the two horse chestnuts you did plant*
*never made it, they just didn't make it, Mary*
*same with the trumpet vine—dead*

the Cape Cod sand, my brother's land
his jealous soil, his fertile hate
everything I planted
grew in a limbo state,
each spring their leaves spread,
opened in rusted hope, shriveled in death, fell

# Dinner at the Diner

a rare steak/dry martini man
my father only once—
my mother sick—
took me to A1 Mac's diner
for dinner
I was thrilled
everything bright, slick
the waitresses so quick
menus thick & filled
with unknown deliciousness—
floats, dogs, frappes, clubs, BLT's
doubles and sides
charmed by the sound of -ettes
I ordered
chicken croquettes
but when I tasted
those fried pyramids
a sick, hard loneliness

I did not know
why my mother was sick
later I overheard
whispered—cancer

I still cannot
eat chicken croquettes—
but I order
my mother's favorite
a coffee frappe shaken to oblivion

# Credo

*Credo in Unum Deum…factorem de coeli et terrae visibilium omnium et invisibilium*

—Nicene Creed A.D. 325

my mother and I arrange her sewing box
placing the spooled thread by graded hues, ordering the lace
and rickrack, spooling their strands around our fingers
placing snaps, needles, pins, hooks and eyes in separate spaces
to ward off her death

the long walk of death sharp, touching cell by cell,
as she went from the green wing chair, to the corduroy couch,
to her pale room, to the white-sheeted hospital, inching away
to her death

at twenty, I thought momentarily of her eternity
like her small perfect stitches running endless
the word forever even in perfection ached

even if endlessness dawns and lemon moons to water,
beginning tide slow turning
on violet dreamed, unseen islands,
glass bowls full of blooming becoming

even if forever snow whipped white, slicing magenta,
the cold, the being of metaphysics holding gold, vermilion
against the heat, of inner rooms, silent tolling pyramids
the ochre sphinx knowing heavy,
as the forest panther foot upon foot prowling

and always the blue tide turning
the bird forever skimming rooms of sky
as Technicolor nightmares rock dark sleep,
always the endless ache in the word forever

# Round Pond and Pleasant Bay, Cape Cod

The pond was a nearly perfect circle. It was not totally enclosed by land, but opened at one point forming a stream that in turn entered a large, quiet bay. Standing on the shore of this bay it was just possible to see it melting into the sea along the horizon. Sometimes I would not know which was the ocean and which was the sky. The small beach from which you could see this was often empty. The few people that came to loll on the sand had waked from the gray-shingled beach houses across the road. The beach and the bay, like the small nearby pond, were almost perfect. Yes, this is true.

# My Daughters and I Are Going to Swim

I. Pleasant Bay, Cape Cod

my daughters and I are going to swim
where the ocean could not hold itself
so it poured into the land
filling a goblet, Pleasant Bay

the bay lapped at the shore
we ran and dove in
and opened our eyes to feel
the salt water sting, finned our arms
and took a turn floating
on our backs like cork buoys
closed our eyes, so not to see
and all the time the water loved holding us

Anne floated on her back
the bliss of seeing her buoyant and free
and Abigail swam, the pleasure
of seeing her smooth skimming
zippering through the water

and then on the sand we walked and talked
"Look at this," back and forth
all the little rocks
and picked up chosen shells
cockles, scallops, oysters, silver and gray,
clams, white with purple, quahogs,
iridescent baby feet and conches to hold
to our ears and hear the roar of the ocean
and shells with perfectly placed holes
to make the necklace
that never happens when you go back home

and mostly we sat on the worn, blue beach blanket and sometimes
drew patterns in the sand and then lay back, basking

time to time we watched
the sailboats as they raced
dancing far out in the bay
skipping in the bay
then they turned one boat,

then another—breathing out
fantastic spinnakers—breast of held air
spinnakers that puffed
like pictures of the wind blowing
from the top of storybook pages

slowly we left, hesitating
to leave maybe one last dip
maybe pick up one last shell,
maybe we'd see one more hermit crab


II. Harwich, Cape Cod

the rented cottage, simple
its shingles a sweater of silver gray
from the breath of the salt water's
spray and the gray of the bayberry bush

my Dad alone now and my daughters
holding on to each vacation day

we sat and ate in the yard
walked its edges looking at what grew

then we walked the beach and
my brother kept coming
to the house to do his laundry
the dull rumble of the dryer day after day
and my Dad could walk
(only with his Irish shillelagh and my girls holding him)
to sit on the lawn chair

midmorning my brother would appear
my Dad would ask him please
take this cellophane cigar band
to throw away
my brother would stand and say no
the sharp point of his anger pricking
the luxury of our vacation hours

and it had taken us so long to come,
we boarded the train in Lewistown, Pennsylvania

the train had run and run along the Susquehanna
to New York City and
change trains and wait
and wait in Grand Central or was it the Port Authority
and for hours we sat
next to a young woman sleeping on a bench
her only possession—a hairbrush in a plastic bag

and then the train zipped up the coast
and we read the New Yorker, a long piece on Silvia Plath
and passed it back and forth
and talked and then we laughed and laughed
in the euphoria of a vacation

my brother picked us up in Providence and drove the long arm
of the Cape
and told me this ride was not a gift, we would have to pay


III. Harwichport, Cape Cod

I wanted to lounge outside at a table with a green striped umbrella
and slowly eat steamed clams and drawn
butter and drink rose colored wine in goblets and laugh
or maybe eat near a marina and watch the white yachts docking

in a reach for earlier days, my father drinks his Martinis
and tired bends his head down,
my daughters hand him his shillelagh

the three are together walking
so slowly, one inch at a time—mothers now leading a child


IV. The Chinese Restaurant on Westerly Parkway, State College

it is Abigail's work break
my daughters and I are eating lunch—egg rolls,
wonton soup and chow mein
we are laughing at some silly remembrance
then I laughed and laughed
I couldn't get up, and I couldn't get up and I laughed and laughed
and they are saying Mom and laughing too

a man at the cash register turns and watches and watches
there is always a man watching when my girls and I are together
they look and watch and stare


V. Fall River, Massachusetts

that April they buried my father
and afterwards as if a siren
had singled every one flew, left, gone

the three of us alone now
my girls and I went down to the sea
to see the swans in the inlet
and we walked and ran
woke the sleeping swans,
their necks and heads bent
hovered in swan prayer
we threw crusts of bread
to stir the swans
floating (and it was twilight)
and I took pictures of my girls,
some with their backs half-turned
they fed the swans so medieval-looking
the stone cotton mills rising behind them


VI. State College, Pennsylvania

the conch shells are on the front step
the beach rocks are scattered about

# Dream Cottage

the small shingled cottage
silver grey like shells in the sea
would be mine
I willed it
its round oak kitchen table
the mottled blue tin plates
the old braided rug

I see the walls my sister
painted deep rose-pink
in the yard white pine,
blue hydrangea
always bluer by the sea
I smell the wild roses
finger their round red hips
the hot sand burns my soles
I run to the ocean
throw myself
into the pounding break
of waves
the salt water throbbing
drowning me in happiness

then on an early August morning
sharp knocks on my door
a will—hand-delivered
shattering the dream

II

# Remember

silent dusk and now
the crows one by one
gliding to the trees
until they bloomed
bouquets of black

the sky, the trees were
what I dreamed—
the etchings
of Renaissance German woods
the Dutch winter of Brueghel
that near pain of innocence,
birds, trees, sky, earth

# Memorial Day

my neighbor,
his big feet in sneakers,
hobbles as fast as he can
across the street
breathless with news
his mouth seems huge to me,
he keeps mispronouncing my name
jerking his head up the street
as he almost screams:
*John is dead John killed himself*

now the other neighbors sift from
their houses—shift from foot to foot
one in her striped nightgown
stands in the doorway
and keeps saying, *a suicide*
a Purple Heart Vietnam Vet
stands on his maimed legs and tells us,
*John's Death Mission—*
*for that a man could kill himself—*
*flying a helicopter*
*to hunt, ferry the dead, the mutilated*

inside I wander aimlessly
from room to room
sit and stare out the windows
see that long summer evening
slowly ending

# Bittersweet Vine

needed to be hacked
back hard
to kill its wanderings
its choking other bushes

I asked John
who mowed the lawn
to kill the vine
he didn't say no,
but he never did destroy it
he just mowed the lawn
in his whirlwind way

one day I asked him
again, to kill
the bittersweet
he smiled and touched
one thick, coiling vine,
reminded me that I once
loved its red blood berries
loved them in the dead of winter

during that month of bittersweet talk
his Viet Nam mission of gathering
the dead grew back
strangling his mind
he began plotting his death

# Tuesday after Memorial Day

shadow and sunshine
angling the front lawn
as the son told me his father
had planned his death for a month
to stop the war bursting in his head,
the blood flying, the body parts,
floating in rice paddies,
the constant stench—
how he blew his brains out
to stop the stinking war

# Seeds

but what can I say
John was the happiest guy
stopping his truck, chatting
on and on about
how his yard would be
wonderfully overrun
with morning glories
*everywhere* he said
spreading his arms

he told me how he found a gold
ring as he mowed a lawn
and once, yes, when he opened
the hood of his truck
a rabbit jumped out
and one summer day
he gave me larkspur seeds
do you understand
how many years ago that was

suddenly this spring the larkspurs bloomed
an outrageously violet-purple
"look-at-me" gorgeous spires
smelling softly sweet
blooming so many years after John
drove to the woods
took a gun and blasted his head open

# Peonies

a glass bowl of peonies
flirts of pink petal
long pistils circle,
unable to resist I move my hand
just to barely touch
the stout stamens
they cover my hand
with their golden dust

III

# I Yearn

to return to Fall River, Massachusetts
to see the Taunton River
to cross over its bridge
opening like an alligator's mouth
see ships from exotic ports
to sit at crowded Magoni's Restaurant
where the waitresses are rushing
and I eat chowder, oysters, cinnamon rolls

I yearn to walk
downtown, past
the granite courthouse,
the white clapboard
Quequechan club
its long, railed porch,
its river view
up Main St.
to get lost in the 5 and 10 cent worlds—
of Woolworth's, Grant's, Kresge's
their windows bursting with
gadgets, dishes, donuts, doll's dresses.
to Ste. Anne's Shrine lined
with crutches of the cured
(miracles are easy to understand)

I want to drive to the ocean
run to the water cool, clean,
its foam running over my toes,
walk the beach on the wet, hard sand
look for shells, see sandpipers,
eat clam fritters and fries
stand at the water's edge
look out and out and out

# Before Mike Died

he and I explored the Cape
we thought we discovered them—
that is how happy we were then—
tiny as shells—little summer
cottages in Wellfleet
eight or nine formed a curving
row near the edge of the inlet
looking toward the bay

that day we laughed at the spindle
railed porches like women
holding up aprons
ready to be filled with fruit
and said we'd rent one next summer
and run in the water when the sun beat down
and sit on the beach and eat
and roll over and down whenever
we wanted to dream or sleep

# Waiting for His Death

the dental hygienist after probing,
scraping, picking and polishing
pressed the chair so I rose up—
chirpily asked me
what I was doing for the rest of the day

I did not tell her that
my friend was dying
that Jim was dying
I did not tell her that
maybe at that moment he was dead
maybe in a few hours he would die
maybe by tomorrow or the next day or the next he will have died

I did not tell her that a nurse with delicate hands
had removed the tubes from his still body
on Sunday and now it was Monday

I did not tell her that there was no more probing for his veins
I did not tell her that there was no more hoping for a look
I did not tell her how I wanted him to say my name —
I did not tell her that maybe he would not, could not
breathe alone

I did not tell her that before I came
I tried to draw flowers I had placed in a blue jar
I did not tell her that I held an artist eraser
in my other hand as I drew
I did not tell her that the eraser was gray and rectangular
a small box-like shape, soft to touch
an eraser that left no trace of any mark

I did not tell her I wanted to keep the small gray eraser perfect
I did not tell her I did something a child would do

49

I didn't tell her that I zipped the eraser into a small, airtight bag
I did not tell her that I put it in a small box, hid it under my bed

I did not tell her that I wanted (God help me)
to be able to hold his death

# The First Week

*—for Lane*

dulled, muted, I sit in the room
at the open window, the lace
breathes in and out

it has been a whole week
a Sunday to Sunday since his death

I remember his garden on the edge
of the stone path filled with
basils, parsley, chives and one begonia

tulips he planted in a blurt
of color under the tree
the wildflowers beyond, the rose wandering

and on the kitchen table
the glass bowl filled with peonies
so pale, so pink they ached

# Every day now I remember you

how I met you in the Paris painting studio
how we walked together down the bent street
to the small café angled on the corner like a movie set,
across from the Luxembourg Gardens

the waiter with a white apron to his toes
holding high his tray
serving us like royalty
no one there but us—laughing
just the edge of love,
a slight swelling of the heart then
the parting, the plans to meet

every day now I remember
as I left you for the first time
walking through the great, ornate gate
promise propelling my steps

I remember first steps into the royal garden
through the side entrance from Rue Vavin
the sprinkled light through the trees
like light shaken through a gold sieve,

the first steps into the park
when my body filled with the
welling of loving
all these years later
remembering those steps, that loving

# Some days I try

to make myself
believe that I do
not miss him
I tell myself
that he treaded so close
to not telling me
what was true
but then I remember
his thick curly hair

and then I begin again
and again, to tell myself,
he would love the orange skies
of summer thunder storms
the grey upon grey
and hidden blue
of November

I tell myself
how we loved
to distraction and despair
he would get lost driving—
whenever he thought of us
I would feel him
coming towards me

and when we became untangled
almost in slow motion—
hand by hand—arm by arm
yet, all the while we clasped
the long unbreakable
thread of want

# I miss the twilight nights

when I could step
noiselessly
into the garden
believing I could
see each new leaf,
see tomatoes tiny as peas
their slightest fuzzed leaves
everywhere their aroma
and wild cucumber corkscrewed
up the cosmos
in thrilled abandon

I miss the evening
smell of the soil
maybe a soft breeze
maybe a cat walking
through the next yard
now darkness descends
so soon, so early
so slow the fading of the light

# Moon Memories

my mother
baked orange cake
with real zest
round, mellow, perfect
my daughter said she tamed
a wild, brown rabbit
that cautiously hopped
in the light of the new moon
my younger daughter told me
she saw waxwings feed
each other hawthorn berries
as they sat close in a tree
as the moon shone pale
in the day blue sky

# Daisy Fleabane

on a spring evening
I snitched daisy fleabane
from the nature meadow
no one will miss her
small white innocence

she is alone now
in a glass vase
in my stark kitchen
far from her field

the world darkens
she wraps her petals
slowly
around her sun center
she becomes a pale violet
small, exotic, erotic
completely alone

# About the Author

Mary Shay McGuire lives in the center of Pennsylvania and was originally from Fall River, Massachusetts. She graduated from Newton College of the Sacred Heart, which is now part of Boston College. After graduating, she studied painting in Paris at the Académies Julian, Grande Chaumière, and Lhôte. She graduated with an MFA in Writing Poetry from The Pennsylvania State University and lives in State College, where she writes and teaches painting.